walks around

Packwood House and Baddesley Clinton

Peter Carbin

Illustrations by Linton Harrison

Published by The National Trust Solihull Centre

Illustrations and maps by Linton Harrison
Photographs by Peter Carbin
Design and production by Richard Winifield

First published in 2017 by The National Trust Solihull Centre

ISBN 978-0-9957778-0-4

www.SolihullNT.org.uk
www.Facebook.com/SolihullNT/

Contents

Disclaimer: the author and publisher have used their best efforts in preparing this text. However, footpaths and landmarks can change with time. The author and publisher shall not be liable for any loss or damages, including but not limited to incidental, consequential or other damages.

Message from our Chairman:

The NT Solihull Centre exists to promote the National Trust, to raise funds for NT projects, national and local, and to give an opportunity for members of our group to meet up at the various activities we organise.

As well as monthly talks, walks and rambles, outings to other NT properties, activities for families and other social events, we offer exclusive "behind the scenes" tours of NT properties.

Proceeds from the sale of this book go to the National Trust Coastline Appeal.

Best wishes

Mark

Mark Kershaw – NT Solihull Centre Chairman

Introduction

This book of walks was originally produced by the National Trust Solihull Centre in 1995 as a project to celebrate the centenary of the National Trust and 21 years of the Solihull Centre. 21 years on both institutions are still going strong.

During that time there have been many changes in the landscape. So all the walks have had to be rewritten. Many changes have been for the better, with footpaths better maintained and with fewer stiles. However, there also are fewer songbirds, butterflies and bees; an indication that the work of the National Trust and other conservation bodies has never been more important.

The Solihull Centre has always been a very active support group, with a current membership of around 500. Over the years it has raised about £300,000 for the National Trust, with our local properties, Baddesley Clinton and Packwood House, both major beneficiaries.

These properties nestle 2½ miles apart in an area of Warwickshire which has changed somewhat since the young Edith Holden enjoyed its rural charms. The centre of Birmingham is less than 15 miles away and the conurbation continues to creep ever closer. Just to the south the M40 has spoilt the Tapster Valley. Overhead ever more aircraft file into Birmingham Airport. Despite this our two properties remain enclosed in a pleasantly varied pastoral landscape, which is very popular with walkers, who can still enjoy its rural charms.

Both Baddesley Clinton and Packwood House are now visited more than ever before. Opening hours are longer and the Trust has created walks around both surrounding estates. Car Parks have been extended and more facilities provided.

Increased car use has made cycling and walking more hazardous around the roads and lanes of the area, and particular care is needed where no pavement is provided.

Both Baddesley Clinton and Packwood House are now visited more than ever before. Opening hours are longer and the Trust has created walks around both surrounding estates. Car Parks have been extended and more facilities provided.

Both properties are signed from the A4141 Warwick Road at Chadwick End and the B4439 at Lapworth. The car park at Packwood is off the lane running through the property, just north of the House. For the car park at Baddesley Clinton take the left fork after the cattle grid on the main drive.

We hope you enjoy these circular walks, which are of varying lengths to suit your available time.

Useful websites:

National Trust Walks: www.nationaltrust.org.uk/walking.

The National Trust Solihull Centre: www.solihullnt.org.uk.

The Heart of England Way Association: www.heartofenglandway.org.

The Millennium Way: www.walking.41club.org.

The Canals and Rivers Trust: www.canalrivertrust.org.uk.

Walks from Baddesley Clinton

Baddesley Clinton, a mediaeval moated manor house, was for centuries quiet and secluded in its surrounding parkland. The home of the Ferrers family for over 500 years it was donated to the National Trust in 1980. It now sees nearly 200,000 visitors a year, and millions around the world have seen it as a setting for the Sherlock Holmes adventure *The Musgrave Ritual,* and the Antiques Roadshow. It can be very busy but it still retains a unique atmosphere.

A walk around the grounds takes a few minutes but is very rewarding. You can take the path over the wooden bridge and around the lake. This leads back alongside the wildflower meadow to the gardens. It is worth widening this walk to see the fish ponds and to take the short woodland walk to the north of the lake. Take a detour also to see the kitchen garden, which is always full of interest in the summer months

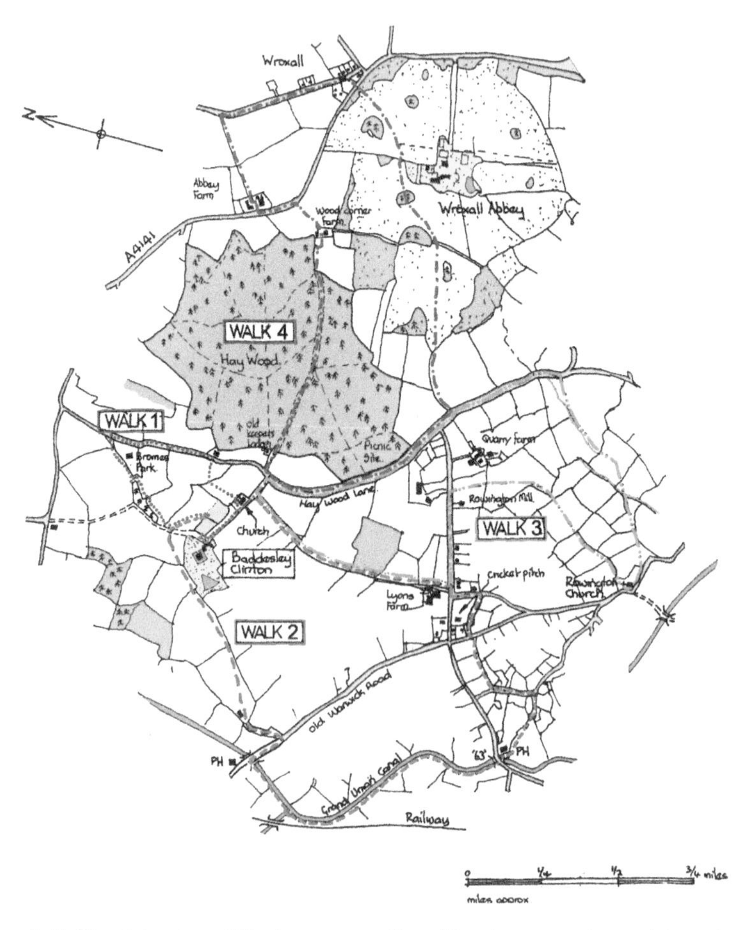

To visit Baddesley Clinton over the Easter weekend (and possibly other busy dates) you need to book in advance. For up to date news, opening times, admission prices, events and information about the property visit the website

www.nationaltrust.org.uk/baddesley-clinton.

1. St Michael's Church

1 mile/30 minutes

St Michael's Church Baddesley Clinton

A large number of visitors to Baddesley Clinton find time to visit the parish church of St. Michael, set in splendid isolation in a churchyard where the spring flowers take their turn to dominate.

Most visitors will stroll up Church Walk, which starts just before the property entrance coming from the car park. For those with a little more time to spare this walk will take you about 30 minutes, along footpaths and a quiet lane, returning from the Church to the House along Church Walk. The original mediaeval deserted village of Baddesley Clinton is thought to have been in this area.

The walk starts from the top area of the car park at Baddesley Clinton. In the lower left hand hedge is an information board about the Estate Walk, and beside it a small gate leading to the field beyond. Go through and turn left, aiming for the bottom left hand corner of the field, walking roughly parallel to the lower car park and drive. In the corner take the smaller of the two wooden gates onto the drive, and turn right.

Just beyond where the two drives meet, and set back a few yards to the right of the cattle grid, is a metal kissing gate. This leads to a path which is part of the Heart of England Way, a long distance footpath linking Cannock Chase to Bourton on the Water (www.heartofenglandway.org).

The path meanders beside a thicket on the left to a stile and plank bridge. Turning right the path continues beside a large field. Beyond a metal kissing gate continue ahead for a short distance to another metal gate leading to Hay Wood Lane. Turn right here past the gates to Bromes Park, and follow the narrow lane. Keep a look out for traffic.

After a few minutes you will come to an isolated house behind a low brick wall with railings. Opposite the house, just before the drive, is a stile. Cross and go over a second stile into the field beyond. This field has been planted with new trees. Go ahead in the gap between the plantations and you will find a stile ahead to the right of a telegraph pole.

Cross the stile, a plank bridge and a second stile. Straight ahead is St. Michael's Church.

(At this point, if you wish to go straight back to the car park, go half right and through the gate half way along the right hand hedge. You will then see two telegraph poles supporting a transformer, and in the gap between them is the gate back into the car park).

Continue up to the church and over a four-step stile into the churchyard. Go right of the tower and turn right on the path through the little gate which leads via Church Walk to the House and car park.

2. Lapworth Canal Walk

4 miles/2 hours

Kingswood Basin

It is said that Birmingham has more miles of canal than Venice. Well the parish of Lapworth is not far behind. Having made their own way from the centre of Birmingham the Grand Union Canal and the Stratford upon Avon canal extend a short arm to meet at Kingswood Basin, before going their separate ways again.

On this walk we take in a stretch of the Grand Union Canal, not only a waterway but also a long distance path from Birmingham to London. Over 200 years old it is the quietest of the three parallel means of transport running south from Lapworth to Warwick. Almost as unobtrusive, the railway shares with the canal periods of inactivity even in mid-summer. Of the M40 the less said the better. The walk is along footpaths, lanes and the canal towpath. It can be muddy in places.

The walk starts from the top area of the Baddesley Clinton car park. In the lower left hand hedge is an information board about the Estate Walk, and beside it a small gate leading to the field beyond. Go through and turn left, aiming for the bottom left hand corner of the field, walking roughly parallel to the lower car park and drive. In the corner take the smaller of the two wooden gates onto the main drive. Opposite, where the drive from the House joins, is a small gate. Go through into the field where just on the right is an 18th century brick lined carriage wash.

Your way lies ahead to meet the boundary fence to the grounds of Baddesley Clinton by a ditch with a pond on your left. Through the gate follow the fence to a metal kissing gate in the bottom corner of the field.

Cross the stream and continue with the fence/hedge on your left, passing wooden gates where the Estate Walk crosses your path. In the next corner by the National Trust sign go through a metal kissing gate. Keep by the hedge for 50 yards then go half right towards the large brick building. You may be assisted here by temporary fencing to show the path between paddocks on either side. Beyond power lines the path leads into a yard by the brick building. Go ahead to exit by a white gate onto a drive leading to the road. Turn right here along the verge to the canal bridge by the Navigation Inn. This is the Grand Union Canal. Cross the road carefully and go down steps on the far side of the bridge. Turn right and follow the tow path south.

Tom o' the Wood pub

You soon come to a bridge over the short arm leading to Kingswood Basin and the Stratford Canal. Continue ahead for half a mile. Leave the canal at the second bridge you come to, bridge 63. Cross over the bridge and, just before the Tom o' the Wood pub (named after a now vanished windmill) take the stile on the right into the grounds of Wharf Cottage. Pass in front of the house and take the metal gates beyond. Walk up the side of the field to a gate in the hedge leading onto the drive from Field Cottage. Follow the drive until it reaches a lane. Turn left past Hickecroft. After about 200 yards take the kissing gate on your right by Millpool Cottage. Follow the enclosed path then go along the right hand side of two fields to exit through a metal kissing gate onto the road.

Cross over with care and walk along The Avenue. Turn left at the end and walk alongside the cricket ground to a T junction. Turn right, then after a few yards take the signed bridleway through a metal gate on your left. This is part of the Heart of England Way. Go ahead and pass the farm on your left. Beyond a metal gate you join a track. After passing a copse on your right, go straight ahead through a small metal gate into a field. Baddesley Clinton Church can be seen ahead as you go down the left hand hedge.

Beyond a metal gate you join the Estate Walk. Cross the next meadow, over the stream. On the right is a small natural play area. With a pond visible behind a fence on your right go through a metal gate in the corner and up the field edge beyond. At the top go through another metal gate then left along the path leading via a kissing gate into the churchyard. Follow the path around to exit by a small gate into Church Walk. This path leads you to the entrance to Baddesley Clinton House, and the car park is just down the drive on the right.

Local pubs: The Navigation at Kingswood and the Tom o' the Wood at Rowington

3. Rowington

4 miles/2 hours

St Lawrence Church, Rowington

Rowington was once a clearing in the Forest of Arden. Now a scattered village, it has a number of large, exclusive houses reflecting its desirable location, but it remains unspoilt.

This walk takes you to St. Lawrence's Church at Rowington, a Grade I listed building dating in parts from the 12th century. The return is along a stretch of the Heart of England Way. This is a long distance footpath crossing the Midlands from north of Cannock Chase to Bourton on the Water.

The walk is along lanes and footpaths. The footpaths can be muddy at times, and there are a couple of moderate slopes.

From the car park at Baddesley Clinton go towards the entrance, then left up Church Walk. Beyond the churchyard take the wide track ahead out to Hay Wood Lane. Turn right and follow the lane for about ¾ mile, past the roadside parking area for Hay Wood and the turning for Rowington and Lapworth. Rounding a left hand bend, just before a road junction on the left, take a stile on your right.

Pick up the right hand hedge ahead. A kissing gate leads into the next field. Here turn right and follow the field edge. Ignore the stile and bridge on your right as you turn the corner, and continue alongside a stream until you come to a second stile and bridge. Cross here, and in the next field go half left, aiming for a bend in the hedge ahead to the right of a brick cottage beyond. Go through the metal kissing gate and follow the hedge to a gate and stile by a tree. From here, aim half right to a kissing gate half way along the bottom fence of the churchyard. A path leads up the left hand side of the church.

Your return to Baddesley Clinton along the Heart of England Way starts from a stile tucked away on the other side of the church, opposite the tower. Over the stile go ahead below the house to a stile opposite. Cross and go right. Beyond the next gateway follow the right hand hedge, but where it turns continue ahead along the line of five trees to a kissing gate beyond.

Cross and go ahead down the field towards a metal gate in the bottom hedge. Through the gate continue ahead, initially with the hedge on your left. With the farm ahead to your right aim just to the left of a telegraph pole by the far hedge. A metal gate will come into view. In the hedge a few yards to its left is a kissing gate. Go through and continue straight ahead. You will see a converted windmill over to your left. At the end of the wooden fence line a metal kissing gate leads to a lane opposite Green Farm.

Turn left here for ¼ mile, past the old windmill and Shakespeare Hall, an early 16th century house, once owned by the Shakespeare family who may or may not have been related to William Shakespeare. Just after the 40 limit sign a footpath and bridle way is signed through a gateway on your right.

Go ahead and pass the farm on your left. Beyond a metal gate you join a track. After passing a copse on your right, go straight ahead through a small metal gate into a field. Baddesley Clinton Church can be seen ahead as you go down the left hand hedge.

Beyond a metal gate you join the Estate Walk. Cross the next meadow, over the stream. On the right is a small natural play area. With a pond visible behind a fence on your right go through a metal gate in the corner and up the field edge beyond. At the top go through another metal gate then left along the path leading via a kissing gate into the churchyard. Follow the path around to exit by a small gate into Church Walk. This path leads you to the entrance to Baddesley Clinton House, and the car park is just down the drive on the right.

4. Wroxall Abbey

4.5 miles/2hrs 30 mins.

St Leonard's Church, Wroxall

Little remains of Wroxall Abbey, a Benedictine nunnery built in the 12th century, but part of the abbey church became the present parish church of St. Leonards. Sir Christopher Wren bought the estate in 1713, but the original Elizabethan house built next to the church was replaced by a Victorian mansion, which is now a luxury hotel. However, Wren may well have designed the unusual curved brick walls of the garden.

Our walk takes you through the surrounding parkland, returning through Hay Wood, once part of the Forest of Arden, and at 200 acres now still a substantial area of woodland.

The walk is along lanes and footpaths. The paths can be muddy at times, particularly in Hay Wood.

Go left from the car park at Baddesley Clinton, and take Church Walk on the left just before the entrance to the House. Go along the path through the churchyard and through two gates, then walk down the wide track beyond to a metal gate at Hay Wood Lane. Turn right here and follow the lane for half a mile. Just beyond the side road signed to Lapworth and Rowington, go through the second metal gate, facing you on the left, signed to Wroxall Abbey 1 mile.

Go left along the field edge. Beyond a solitary tree take the stile on your left. Go straight ahead, aiming for the gap below Wroxall Abbey in the distance. As you get closer you will see, to the right of the tall spinney, two metal gates leading into the next field at a point where the stream is crossed. Beyond the gates go half left up the slope, with cedar trees on your right and aim for a yellow marker post midway along the edge of the copse half left ahead. Here there is a small metal gate leading to a path through the copse and out by another small gate.

In the next field go half right, aiming midway along the gap between the two plantations. To the left of a gateway is a metal kissing gate leading to a stile beyond. Here pick up the track going half left then ahead, taking you to a metal gate and narrow stile to the A4141. Go straight across the road and through an old metal kissing gate. The footpath ahead takes you alongside the fence to a stile and lane. To the right is Wren Hall, which does excellent teas on a summer Sunday afternoon. Your way is left along the lane for about a quarter of a mile. Pass a small cemetery, then just beyond a gentle right curve take the track on your left through a metal gate.

This bridleway leads directly to the farm ahead. Go into the farmyard through metal gates, then beyond the brick building curve left, then between brick walls for a few yards to the road. Turn left along the pavement for about 150 yards. After the '50' sign there is a lane opposite. Cross with care and follow this short lane. You will come to a gateway, flanked by brick pillars with two rather cross birds of prey. Follow round to the left, past the entrance to Hay Wood Grange. Ahead is a metal gate. Go right here by a public bridleway post and through the smaller metal gate. After the fence and barn a further metal gate leads into a field, bordered ahead by Hay Wood.

Go right for a short distance, and a sign then points you to the bottom right hand corner of the field. Here you enter the wood. Swing left on the track ahead, and follow it for some distance through the woods, crossing straight over when a main track is met at a crossroads. You emerge from the wood by the grounds to a modern, wooden panelled house. Go left and then right along a driveway to Hay Wood Lane. Immediately opposite is the track and path leading back through the churchyard to Baddesley Clinton.

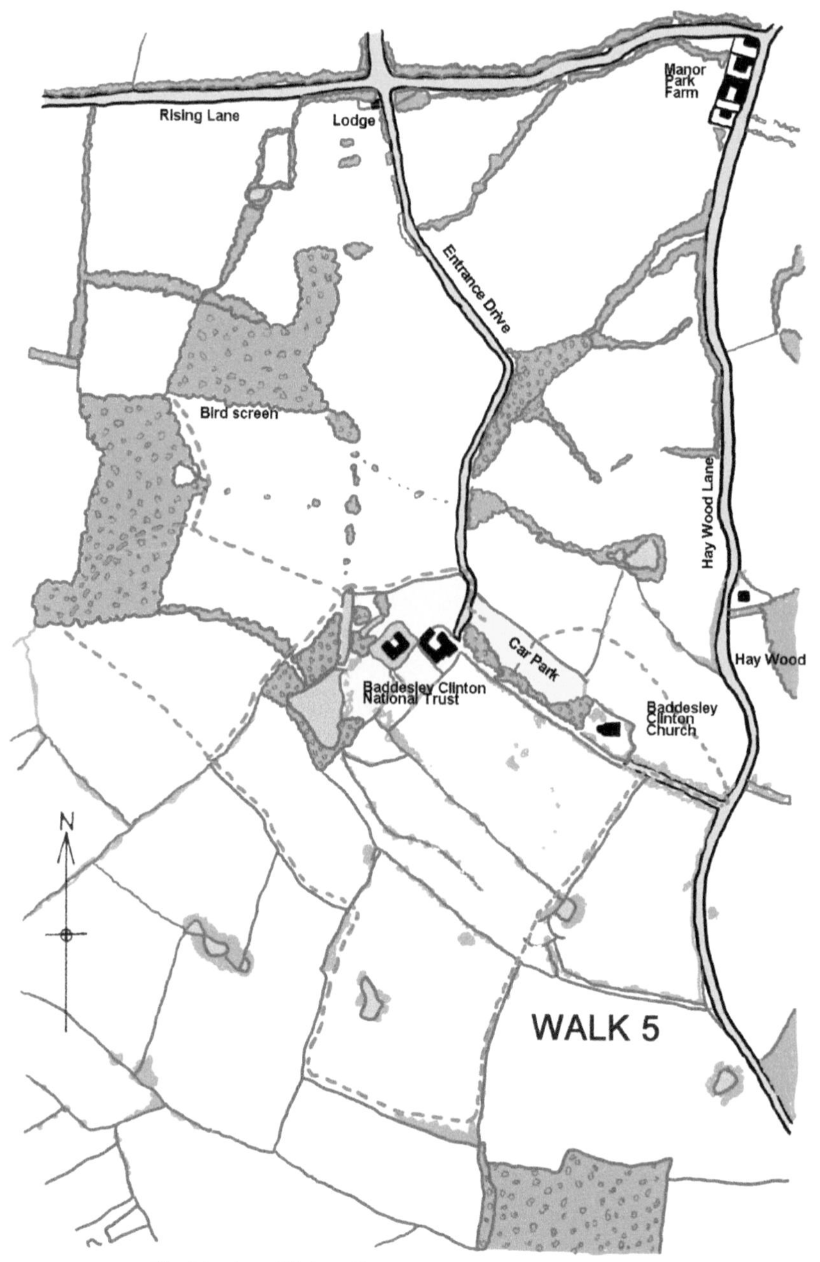

Baddesley Clinton Estate Walk

5. Baddesley Clinton Estate Walk

1¾ miles/ 50 minutes

Sheep on the estate walk

This walk around the fields and woods of the Baddesley Clinton Estate can also be found on a National Trust walks card, which you can obtain from Reception at the entrance to the property. The route is way marked by orange arrows.

Generally ground conditions are good, but there may be muddy spots after rain.

The walk starts from a small wooden gate near the bottom left hand corner of the top car park at Baddesley Clinton. In the field go right past the two telegraph poles, aiming to the left of the next telegraph pole by the hedge, where there is a gateway. Go through the small gate and cross the large field towards the right hand corner. Hay Wood is visible ahead, with Baddesley Clinton Church on your right.

In the corner of the field a metal kissing gate leads out onto Hay Wood Lane. Take the track on your right towards the church, but on meeting the two gates go left through the metal gate by the National Trust sign. Go down the field with the hedge on your left to a metal gate. Go through and beyond the small natural play area cross the stream by the small bridge. At this point there is a fork in the path ahead. To the left the Heart of England Way continues towards Rowington. Your way is to the right and through a metal kissing gate. In the next field follow the path ahead with the hedge on your left.

At the top of the field ignore the gap and continue around now with a spinney on your left. By a wooden bench join the track which runs next to the hedge. Continue past wooden gates in the next corner to go down the 3rd edge of this field, along a clear path which goes left of a small spinney to a wooden gate. Go through and again follow the left hand hedge all the way down this field until you meet wooden gates by an oak tree. Go through, and you can take a half mile short cut here if you wish.

(To do so go right and down to the corner. Take the kissing gate and continue ahead. From a further kissing gate close to the House grounds go half left to meet the main drive. Go right back to the car park).

The Estate Walk continues along the raised path down the middle of the field ahead. This leads to a gate into a wood. Take the right hand path ahead, which meanders through the wood until you reach an exit gate into a field. Go straight ahead along the mown path to a wooden fence and gate close to the perimeter of the House grounds. Go through and then half left, still along the clear path which leads to the main drive via a wooden gate. As you near the gate you will see on the left an 18th century carriage wash.

The drive leads to the lower car park and entrance to the House. To return to the top car park cross over and go through the wooden gate on your right into the field. With the drive on your right cut the corner and pass to the right of a large chestnut tree. Aim for the two telegraph poles where you will find the small gate leading back into the car park.

Walks from Packwood House

Packwood House was given to the National Trust in 1941 by Graham Baron Ash. Both the house and the gardens reflect his restoration work and collections. The property was previously occupied by the Featherstone family, yeoman farmers who had lived at Packwood House since it was built in the 15th century.

Packwood is justifiably famous for its gardens, and the sculpted yews representing the Sermon on the Mount. It has a lovely walk around the lake, through woodland and parkland, with attractive views back across to the House.

There is a kitchen garden, café, shop and plant sales.

At the time of publication Packwood is closed on Mondays in January and February, and on 24th and 25th December. Over the Easter weekend pre booking is required. For the up to date opening times, admission prices and events, and lots of information about the property visit the web site:

www.nationaltrust.org.uk/packwood-house.

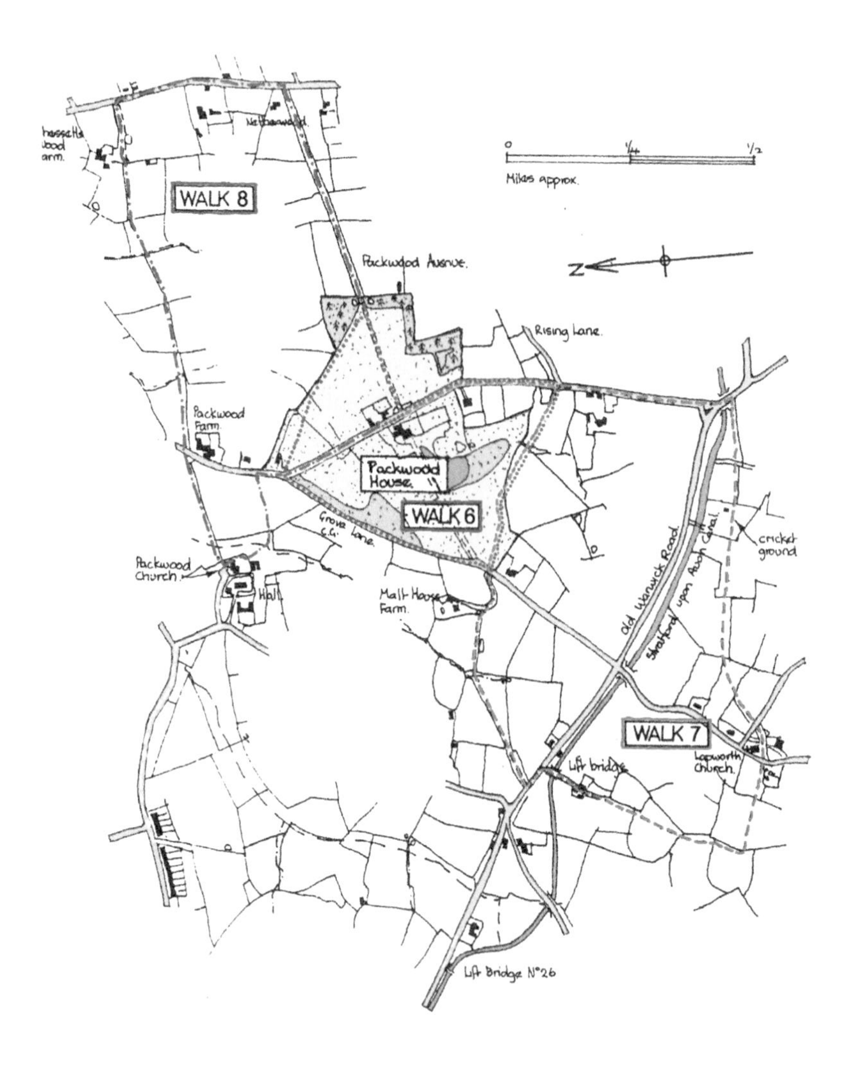
WALK 8
0
1/4
1/2
Miles approx.
Packwood Avenue.
N
Rising Lane.
Packwood Farm.
Packwood House.
WALK 6
Grove C.G. Lane
Packwood Church.
Hall
Malt House Farm.
Old Warwick Road.
Stratford upon Avon Canal.
cricket ground
WALK 7
Lapworth Church.
Lift bridge
Lift Bridge N°26

6. Packwood Grounds

1¾ miles/1 hour

On this walk we enjoy a short stretch of the Avenue before we circle the property, enjoying the surrounding parkland and with good views of the lake and the House beyond.

There are likely to be sheep grazing in the park. The walk is along footpaths and lanes. There may be some mud after heavy rain, and the final stretch of lane back to Packwood House can be quite busy with cars, especially on a Sunday afternoon.

Start off by going up the brick steps opposite the main entrance to the House, and through the gate into Packwood Avenue. Follow the Avenue only as far as the first gate. Do not go through, but instead go left and follow the field edge down alongside the copse and past an old iron gate. Aim for the house in the distance.

The Estate Walk goes off to the right but your way is ahead between two trees then over a wooden bridge into the next field. Now head to the left of the house ahead, and a National Trust logo sign will become visible, as will a stile and gate about 30 yards to the left of the house.

Over the stile enter Grove Lane opposite and follow this lane past Hockley Heath Cricket Club and the entrance to Malt House Barns. When the lane swings right, just beyond the columns of the park gate set back on your left, take a kissing gate opposite the entrance to Malt House Farm.

Follow the waymark posts ahead, through trees and to the right of a dip, to pick up the right hand hedge leading to a metal gate into the next field. Go along the left hand hedge beyond. Soon after the hedge turns to run along the bottom of the field look out for a metal gate on the left. This leads over wooden sleepers to a path running up the side of the grounds to a large house ahead. Going past a large pond on your left, the path leads down a couple of steps to a road junction.

Take the lane to your left and follow it back to Packwood House.

7. Lapworth

3½ miles/1¾ hours

Footpath at Lapworth

Lapworth is a large parish with newer development around the canal and railway at Kingswood, not far from Lapworth station. In fact the station was called Kingswood until 1902, and is over a mile from the original village of Lapworth. This is centred around the impressive church of St. Mary, a Grade I listed building dating from the 12th century, which has a raised chapel at the west end, above a processional path.

This walk takes you out to Lapworth church and back to Packwood, along footpaths and lanes. There are a couple moderate slopes. The stretch of lane at the start and end of the walk can be busy, especially on Sundays.

From the car park at Packwood House go left and up the lane for half a mile, continuing ahead at the junction with Rising Lane, and left at the fork, signed to Lapworth and Warwick. Shortly after you reach the main road. Cross over the road and the canal. A few yards on beyond the wooden fence take the metal gate on your right by a canal access point.

Lapworth Cricket Club

Go ahead with the hedge on your left, crossing a small stream in the dip, and up to a kissing gate leading into a cricket field. Go left around the edge, and in front of the scoreboard, to a metal gate in the left hand corner. Two paths diverge here. Follow the one straight ahead to a stile. In the next field continue ahead again down the slope to a gap in the left hand corner. This leads to another metal gate and a path beside a large pond. Waymark posts guide you to a further metal gate. In the next field cross to a stile and gate in the top right hand corner, emerging onto a narrow lane.

Cross over and curve right by the old wooden gate. Follow the path into the churchyard, past the church porch and down steps to the road. A few yards to the right take the stile opposite signed the Millennium Way (a long distance footpath from Pershore to Middleton Cheney). Go down the sloping field, past outbuildings, to a stile and gate in the dip. Continue ahead up the next field, over the rise and down to a metal gate in the next hedge.

Cross the bridge, then turn immediately right alongside the stream. Just past a pond on the left take the stile and follow the lower edge of the next field to another stile between a metal gate and a tree. Go straight ahead up the slope. Between another metal gate and tree take a stile and go ahead towards farm buildings. Go through the metal gate and into the yard. Cross between the cowsheds and the brick cottage and follow the track ahead to a canal lift bridge.

Over the Stratford Canal continue ahead to a main road. Turn left for 75 yards, and just before the blue "weak bridge" sign cross over to a stile in the gateway opposite. Go down the field to a gap ahead. Follow the left hand hedge beyond to a gap at the bottom of the field, then along the right hand edge ahead. In the corner, to the right of the house, cross a stile, go along the left hand edge for a few yards, then take the gap on your left onto the drive by the house gates.

Turn right along the hedged driveway to the lane. Opposite a stile takes you into the parkland of Packwood estate. Follow the waymark posts ahead, through trees and to the right of a dip, to pick up the right hand hedge leading to a metal gate into the next field. Go along the left hand hedge beyond. Soon after the hedge turns to run along the bottom of the field look out for a metal gate on the left. This leads over wooden sleepers to a path running up the side of the grounds to a large house ahead. Going past a large pond on your left, the path leads down a couple of steps to the road junction you passed on the way out.

Take the lane on your left to return to Packwood House.

8. Packwood Church

2½ miles/1¼ hours (just to the church and back is 1 mile/30 minutes)

St Giles Church, Packwood

Packwood Church is some distance from the House, and in fact is situated next to the privately owned Packwood Hall, a moated grange linked to the churchyard by a red brick bridge. The Church is dedicated to St. Giles. Much altered by the Victorians, it dates from the 13th century. It shares with the Church of St. Michael at Baddesley Clinton the legend that the tower was built by Nicholas Brome of Baddesley Clinton in atonement for murdering the priest.

This walk takes you firstly to the Church, then across to Chessetts Wood, returning along the full length of Packwood Avenue. Conditions for the most part are usually quite good, but there can be muddy areas after prolonged rain.

From Packwood House car park turn right and follow the road to a metal kissing gate on the left about 75 yards beyond the junction with Grove Lane. Take the raised track ahead. In the next field continue ahead as far as the stream on your right. Turn half right towards the church, entering the churchyard through a wooden kissing gate in front of the cottage.

Go to the right of the church. In the far corner topped by a sundial is the gravestone of Graham Baron Ash, the last owner of Packwood, and his parents. Just beyond use the wooden kissing gate in the corner to leave the churchyard, then swing right and cross a stream to take up the right hand hedge.

(To return to Packwood House at this point take a stile half way along this hedge, walk ahead and beyond the dip on your left swing left to re-join your outward route at the gate onto the lane).

Keep the same direction in the corner to meet a kissing gate onto a lane. Cross to another kissing gate opposite. Go along the right hand hedge beyond to the corner where two wooden bridges lead you to a short track. Walk up to the metal gates, pushing your way through the small one into the field beyond.

Continue ahead with a wire fence on your left, over the rise and down to a stile and plank bridge in the corner. Turn left in the field and meander around the edge beside the ditch to a stile leading onto a track. Turn right and follow the track around the left bend. As you approach the house go through two metal gates. With the house on your right join the track leading from the farm buildings and follow it past wooden gates and a pond on your right, emerging onto Chessetts Wood Road.

Turn right and follow the road for just over ¼ mile, using the verge if possible as this is a fast road. Just past "Netherwood" a kissing gate on the right leads into Packwood Avenue. Follow it straight down for ½ mile with Packwood House gradually coming into view beyond the two ponds. When you reach the road in front of the House turn right to return to the car park.

9. Packwood Estate Walk

¾ mile/45 minutes

Welly walk

This short walk is ideal for children, and for grown-ups looking for a bit of exercise. It can be muddy, and part of it has in fact been named the "welly walk". More details of the activities for children and a description of the "welly walk" can be found on the National Trust website at www.nationaltrust.org.uk/packwood-house/trails/packwood-welly-walk.

Start off by going up the brick steps opposite the main entrance to the House, and through the gate into Packwood Avenue. Follow the Avenue only as far as the first gate. Do not go through, but instead go left and follow the field edge down alongside the wood until you come to a small wooden gate in the hedge beyond.

Go through and follow a worn path which goes half right in the next field. Two wooden gates then lead through a wide hedge. Beyond, the path meanders via a boardwalk to a gate leading into a wood. Follow the path through the wood to exit beside a pond onto Packwood Avenue.

The Estate Walk continues ahead from beside a second pond, and at this point you are on the "welly walk", and there are various distractions for inquisitive children.

Beyond a wooden gate and plank bridge the walk continues along a clear path past a wooden wigwam. In a clearing keep round to the left. You will see somewhere to sit on a large tree trunk as you follow the winding path. As you come out of the wood there is a field on your right, and an arched wooden gateway leading into it.

Walk parallel to the road, and aim for the finger post at the end of Packwood Avenue. Here you can take the path ahead to the restaurant and reception, or left to the House.

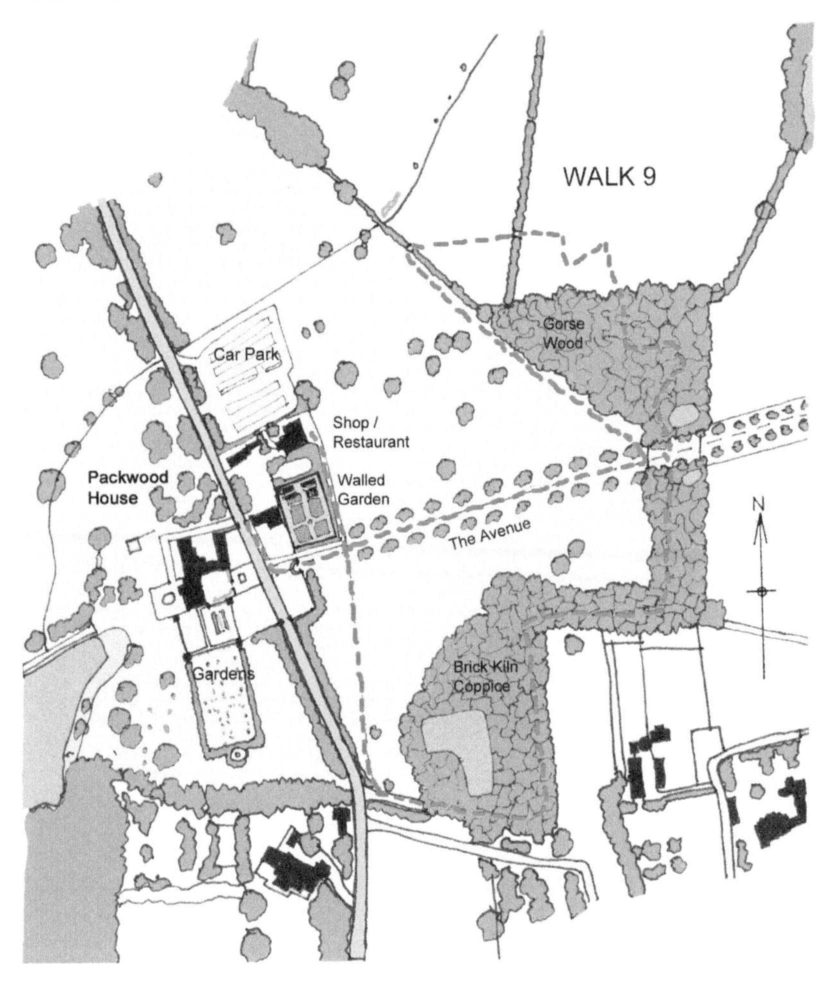
WALK 9
Gorse Wood
Car Park
Shop / Restaurant
Walled Garden
Packwood House
The Avenue
N
Gardens
Brick Kiln Coppice

10. Baddesley Clinton & Packwood

5½ miles/2¾ hours

National Trust Solihull Centre Walking Group

This final walk takes in both properties. Our route description starts at Baddesley Clinton, but you can of course start at Packwood. You can also find this walk, and three others, at: *http://www.nationaltrust.org.uk/baddesley-clinton/lists/walks-at-baddesley-clinton.*

The walk is along roads, footpaths and towpaths. Generally ground conditions are good, but after prolonged rain the field before Rising Lane can get boggy, and there may be some muddy spots elsewhere.

You will walk the length of Packwood Avenue, and also down the Lapworth flight of locks to the busy and popular canal basin at Kingswood.

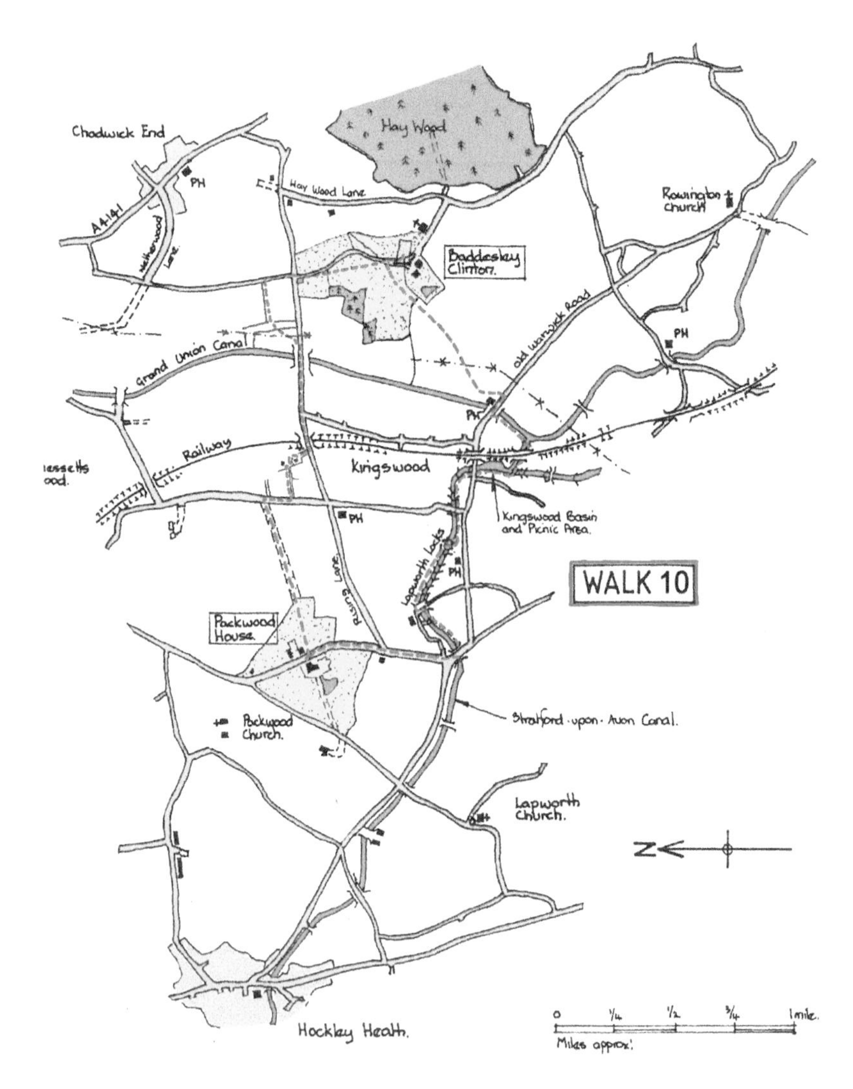

Begin by walking back along the main drive at Baddesley Clinton. Take the small gate to the right of the cattle grid and then cut across the park with the drive curving round to your right. Aim for the lodge where you re-join the drive, just before the main entrance. You come out at a cross roads.

Go straight across into Netherwood Lane, and continue for about 200 yards to a metal gateway on the left.

Follow the right hand hedge down the field then keep ahead over a small plank bridge and through a metal gate. In the next field go half left through a metal kissing gate and under power lines to exit via a gate and sleeper bridge in the far corner.

You emerge onto Rising Lane. Beware of traffic. Turn right over the canal, and continue past Station Road. Just after the railway bridge take the small lane on the right leading to "The Grove". You come to gates just before the house. Here take the footpath on the right and follow it around the perimeter of the property through a kissing gate and alongside a laurel hedge.

Another kissing gate leads to a lane. Opposite and just to the right take the kissing gate and follow the left hand hedge in the field beyond. A metal kissing gate leads to a road. Turn right and where possible keep to the verge. Just past the drive to "Uplands Farm" look for a wooden gate and small metal kissing gate set back on the left. These lead into Packwood Avenue. Follow it straight down for ½ mile with Packwood House gradually coming into view beyond the two ponds.

As you arrive at Packwood House you will see a path on your right leading out to the road. If you want to visit the property and its facilities follow the path the other way back to reception.

To return to Baddesley Clinton turn left on the road in front of the house and continue initially with the yew garden visible on your right. Continue ahead at the junction with Rising Lane, signed to Lapworth. When you reach a fork in the road take the lane ahead signed to Lapworth and Warwick. This soon takes you out onto the B4432 beside a canal bridge.

Cross over and a few yards down take the path by the field gate leading to the Stratford Canal. Turn right and follow the towpath past Lapworth locks and under the B4432 at Bridge 35 to reach Kingswood Canal Basin.

Barrel-roofed cottage

The southern section of the Stratford canal starts here. After being rescued from proposed closure in 1958, this stretch of waterway to Stratford was restored by the National Trust with much volunteer help. In 1964 it was reopened, and was then owned and maintained by the National Trust until 1988 when it passed to British Waterways. It is characterised by barrel roof cottages and split bridges, and one of each is to be seen here at Kingswood Basin.

The Stratford Canal continues ahead but your way lies over a split bridge 36, and left of the cottage, to the short arm which links the Stratford canal with the Grand Union Canal. Bridge 36A is actually quite modern, hence no gap for the horse rope to pass through. Go left, passing under the railway bridge, to the junction with the Grand Union. This canal links London and Birmingham.

Go left over brick bridge 37, and follow the towpath. At the next bridge (65) go up steps to the road. Cross with care, and turn right past *The Navigation* pub. Continue on the verge where possible to a way-marked drive opposite *The Manor House.* Follow the drive to a white gate. Take the adjacent metal kissing gate and cross the stable yard to the right of the brick building. Here a fenced way-marked path goes half right through paddocks and under power cables to meet the right hand hedge.

Beyond a metal kissing gate a National Trust sign marks the perimeter of the Baddesley Clinton Estate. Continue along the right hand hedge, crossing the Estate Walk, and down to the corner. Take the kissing gate and continue ahead. From a further kissing gate close to the House grounds go half left to meet the main drive. Go right back to the car park.

Local Pub: The Navigation at Kingswood

11. National Trust Solihull Centre

We strive to work together with local National Trust properties to make sure the money we raise is going to the causes that need it most.

In over 40 years we have raised nearly £300,000 for National Trust properties and appeal funds.

Our dedicated 'At Risk' Appeals have included funds to restore the Coat of Arms stained glass window and restoration of the drapes on Queen Margaret's Bed at Packwood.

Funds raised from the sale of this book and from our monthly guided walks go to the National Trust Coastline Appeal.

Activities

Behind the scenes privilege tours:

Solihull members have been able to visit properties behind the scenes where the general pubic cannot. We are able to organise visits to properties that are new to the Trust and are undergoing restoration.

Sunday morning walks:

Once a month you can join one of our leisurely three to four mile walks in the local countryside. Our guide leads the group and has you back in time for lunch!

Walks usually take place on the first Sunday of the month and set off at 10.30.

Guest speakers

Our talks and lectures take place twice a month, with a fascinating range of speakers. Both are held at the Methodist Church or church hall in Solihull. The Friday afternoon talks start at 2pm and the Tuesday evening lectures at 7.45pm

Subjects cover a wide range of interest and can be thought provoking, enlightening and humorous. You can inspect the programme on our web site – see opposite.

Tuesday evening lectures:

September to April in Solihull Methodist Church at 19.30.

Friday afternoon talks:

September to April in Solihull Methodist Church Hall at 14.00.

Coach outings:

Our coach outings take the stress out of visiting places of interest slightly further afield. We have an active programme of outings, to National Trust properties and also other gardens, craft centres and historic places.

With pick up points at Solihull and Dorridge they are easily accessible and reasonably priced.

Family activities:

We think it's important to put on events to encourage the whole family to enjoy our National Trust properties. Our hugely popular Teddy Bears' picnic is a highlight of the summer holidays and enjoyed by children, parents and grandparents.

Look out for other activities throughout the year, including nature walks, story telling and crafts.

How to join

Special offer: Join between September and December, and your membership will run to December in the following year.

Single membership: £10

Two people at same address: £15

How to find out more

Please visit our website:

www.SolihullNT.org.uk

Please visit us on Facebook:

www.facebook.com/solihullnt/

Lightning Source UK Ltd.
Milton Keynes UK
UKOW07f1315180517
301484UK00013B/82/P

9 780995 777804